INSPIRING POEMS

INSPIRING POEMS

Compiled by C. B. Eavey

ZONDERVAN PUBLISHING HOUSE

OF THE ZONDERVAN CORPORATION
GRAND RAPIDS, MICHIGAN 49506

INSPIRING POEMS

Copyright © 1970 by
Zondervan Publishing House
Grand Rapids, Michigan

Second printing December 1970
Third printing 1971
Fourth printing 1973
Fifth printing 1974

Library of Congress Catalog Card Number 70-120036

Preface

The purpose of poetry is to create authentic emotion. Since emotion is basic, the source of our thinking and doing and living, poetry expressive of exalted truth has an animating effect on us, influencing us in every aspect of our lives.

This volume of poems was compiled in the conviction that "truth shines the brighter clad in verse." In this era of emphasis on wrong and evil, crime and corruption, delinquency and moral breakdown, rioting and war, there is great need for uplifting emotions with truths that are ennobling, inspiring, and elevating.

Life is far more than a matter of rights and political doctrines, dresses and suits, houses and furnishings, bank accounts and bonds, gadgets and knick-knacks, and the endless number of other things, large and small, that men ceaselessly stretch themselves to get. Thus we need truths to cling to, truths that feed the soul and the spirit, truths that are concerned with the unseen realities of a life that is not nourished by the everyday aspects of this mortal existence. In these disturbing times we need truths that alleviate fears, encourage us to simple deep faith in God, inspire us to attainment of the best of which we are capable, and stimulate us to living on a high moral level.

The poems herein were not chosen for their literary excellence but for the appeal they make to the high and noble feelings of the human heart. The principle governing the search for them was not that of mere beauty, but that of finding words that point the soul to God in whom alone we have sufficiency, words that uplift the spirit and bring comfort, words that encourage and challenge, words that have vital meaning to the reader.

C. B. EAVEY

INDEX

INSPIRING POEMS

The Best Memory System

Forget each kindness that you do
As soon as you have done it;
Forget the praise that falls to you
The moment you have won it;
Forget the slander that you hear
Before you can repeat it;
Forget each slight, each spite, each sneer
Whenever you may meet it.

Remember every kindness done
To you, whate'er its measure;
Remember praise by others won
And pass it on with pleasure;
Remember every promise made
And keep it to the letter;
Remember those who lend you aid
And be a grateful debtor.

Remember all the happiness
That comes your way in living;
Forget each worry and distress,
Be hopeful and forgiving;
Remember good, remember truth,
Remember heaven's above you,
And you will find through age and youth
True joy, and hearts to love you.

— Author unknown

Right Choosing

In all earth's places you are right
To choose the best you can
Provided that you do not try
To crowd some other man.

— Dickens

Feelings and the Word

For feelings come and feelings go
  And feelings are deceiving;
My warrant is the Word of God,
  Naught else is worth believing.

Though all my heart should feel condemned
  For want of some sweet token,
There is One greater than my heart
  Whose Word cannot be broken.

I'll trust in God's unchanging Word
  Till soul and body sever,
For, though all things shall pass away
  His Word shall stand forever.

— Martin Luther

MYSELF

I have to live with myself, and so
I want to be fit for myself to know;
I want to be able, as days go by,
Always to look myself straight in the eye;
I don't want to stand with the setting sun
And hate myself for the things I've done.

I don't want to keep on a closet shelf
A lot of secrets about myself,
And fool myself as I come and go,
Into thinking nobody else will know
The kind of man I really am;
I don't want to dress myself in sham.

I want to go out with my head erect,
I want to deserve all men's respect;
And here in the struggle for fame and pelf
I want to be able to like myself;
I don't want to look at myself and know
That I'm bluster and bluff and empty show.

I never can hide myself from me;
I see what others may never see;
I know what others may never know;
I never can fool myself and so
Whatever happens, I want to be
Self-respecting and conscience free.

— *Author unknown*

As Thy Days

Why should I fear lest by their weight
Tomorrow's tasks should prove too great?
I know my Father will not ask
Me to perform a greater task
Than He will give me strength to do:
For in His precious Word so true,
He there has promised you and me,
That "As thy days, thy strength shall be."

— *Selected*

O Love Divine

O Love Divine! that stooped to share
Our sharpest pang, our bitterest tear,
On Thee we cast each earth-born care,
We smile at pain, while Thou art near.

Though long the weary way we tread,
And sorrow crown each lingering year,
No path we shun, no darkness dread,
Our hearts still whispering, Thou art near.

On Thee we fling our burdening woe,
O Love Divine, forever dear;
Content to suffer while we know
Living or dying, Thou art near!

— *O. W. Holmes*

PRAYER

I know not by what methods rare,
But this I know: God answers prayer.
I know not when He sends the word
That tells us fervent prayer is heard.
I know it cometh soon or late;
Therefore, we need to pray and wait.
I know not if the blessing sought
Will come in just the guise I thought.
I leave my prayers with Him alone
Whose will is wiser than my own.

— Selected

THE BEAUTY OF DUTY

The longer on this earth we live
And weigh the various qualities of men,
The more we feel the high, stern-featured beauty
Of plain devotedness to duty.
Steadfast and still, nor paid with mortal praise,
But finding amplest recompense
For life's ungarlanded expense
In work done squarely and unwasted days.

— Lowell

THE PRECIOUS CHRIST

Sweet is the thought of Jesus,
   It makes our hearts o'erflow;
But sweeter is His presence
   Than all things here below.

No music half so tuneful
   Can strike upon our ear.
No thought is so delightful
   As Jesus' name most dear.

Hope-giver to the contrite,
   To those who call how kind!
How gracious to the seeking!
   But what to those who find?

Thou art the heart's best rapture,
   The mind's true life and light;
Exceeding every pleasure,
   Surpassing all delight.

— Bernard of Clairvaux

This Day

This day is mine to mar or make,
   God keep me strong and true;
Let me no erring by-path take,
   No doubtful action do.

Grant me when the setting sun
   This day shall end,
I may rejoice o'er something done,
   Be richer by a friend.

Let all I meet along the way
   Speak well of me tonight.
I would not have the humblest say
   I'd hurt him by a slight.

Let there be something true and fine,
   When night slips down, to tell
That I have lived this day of mine
   Not selfishly, but well.

— Selected

Be Pleasant

We cannot, of course, all be handsome,
 And it's hard for us all to be good,
We are sure now and then to be lonely,
 And we don't always do as we should.
To be patient is not always easy,
 To be cheerful is much harder still,
But at least we can always be pleasant,
 If we make up our minds that we will.
And it pays every time to be kindly,
 Although you feel worried and blue;
If you smile at the world and look cheerful,
 The world will soon smile back at you.
So try to brace up and look pleasant,
 No matter how low you are down;
Good humor is always contagious,
 But you banish your friends when you frown.

— *Selected*

NEVER GIVE UP

Never give up! it is wiser and better
  Always to hope, than once to despair;
Fling off the load of doubt's cankering fetter,
  And break the dark spell of tyrannical care.

Never give up! or the burdens may sink you;
  Providence kindly has mingled the cup,
And in all trials or troubles, bethink you,
  The watchword of life must be, Never give up.

Never give up! there are chances and changes
  Helping the hopeful a hundred to one;
And through the chaos High Wisdom arranges
  Ever, success — if you'll only hope on.

Never give up! for the wisest is boldest,
  Knowing that Providence mingles the cup,
And of all maxims the best, as the oldest,
  Is the true watchword, Never give up!

Never give up! though the grape-shot may rattle,
  Or the full thunder-cloud over you burst;
Stand like a rock, and the storm and the battle
  Little shall harm you, though doing their worst.

Never give up! if adversity presses,
  Providence wisely has mingled the cup,
And the best counsel in all your distresses
  Is the stout watchword, Never give up!

— *M. F. Tupper*

BETTER THAN SACRIFICE

If I would for Jesus live,
And my service freely give,
First of all I hear Him say
All His servants must obey.

Or, if bravely I would fight,
Striving hard to do the right,
And to follow day by day,
Still I must His word obey.

Could I bring to Jesus gold,
Just as much as I could hold,
Still for all He would not care
If obedience was not there.

Could I fill my hands with gems
Fit for monarch's diadems,
Jesus still would turn away
If my heart could not obey.

Not like prophets need we preach,
Need not learn an angel's speech,
Nor, like martyrs, face the fires —
'Tis obedience Christ desires.

Let me serve with loving heart,
Let me act a valiant part;
But before I praise and pray,
May I first my Lord obey.

— Selected

Shining

In the world is darkness,
    So we must shine,
You in your little corner,
    And I in mine.

— *Selected*

Our Little Worries

The little worries that we meet each day
May lie as stumbling-blocks across our way;
Or we may make them stepping-stones to be
Nearer each day, O Lord, our God, to Thee!

— *Selected*

KINDNESS

How softly on the bruised heart
   A word of kindness falls,
And to the dry and parched soul
   The moistening teardrop calls.
Oh! if they knew who walked the earth,
   Mid sorrow, grief and pain,
The power a word of kindness hath,
   'T were Paradise again.

The wealthiest and the poorest may
   The simple pittance give,
And bid delight to withered hearts
   Return again alive.
Oh! what is life, if love be lost,
   If man's unkind to man.
Oh! what the heaven that waits beyond
   This brief and mortal span.

As stars upon the tranquil sea
   In mimic glory shine
So words of kindness in the heart
   Reflect the source divine.
Oh! then be kind, whoe'er thou art
   That breathest mortal breath,
And it shall brighten all thy life
   And sweeten even death.

— Selected

LET BUT THE HEART BE BEAUTIFUL

Let but the heart be beautiful
  And I care not for the face,
I heed not that the form may want
  Pride, dignity or grace.
Let the mind be filled with glowing thoughts
  And the soul with sympathy,
And I care not if the cheek be pale
  Or the eye lack brilliancy.

What though the cheek be beautiful,
  It soon must lose its bloom,
The eyes' bright luster soon will fade,
  In the dark and silent tomb:
But the glory of the mind will live
  Though the joyous life depart
And the magic charm can ne'er decay
  Of a true and nobler heart.

The thoughts that utter gentle words
  Have a beauty all their own,
And more I prize a kindly voice
  Than music's sweetest tones,
And though its sounds are harsh and shrill,
  If the heart within beats free,
And echoes back each glad impulse
  'Tis all the world to me.

— Selected

The Oldest Christian Hymn

Shepherd of tender youth,
Guiding in love and truth,
  Through devious ways;
Christ, our triumphant King,
Join we Thy name to sing
And our dear children bring,
  Shouting Thy praise.

Most high and holy Lord,
Glorious, revealing Word,
  Healer of strife
Thou didst Thyself abase
That from sin's deep disgrace
Thou mightest save our race,
  Giving us life.

Thou art our great High Priest;
Thou hast prepared the feast
  Of holy love.
In all our sin and pain,
None call on Thee in vain,
Help Thou dost not disdain,
  Help from above.

Ever be near our side,
All wise and mighty Guide,
  Our staff and song.
Jesus! thou Christ of God!
Taught by Thy living word,
Lead us where Thou hast trod
  Make our faith strong.

So now, and till we die,
Sound we Thy praises high
    And joyful sing.
With all the holy throng,
Who to Thy church belong,
Join we to swell the song
    To Christ our King.

— *From the third book of Clement
of Alexandria*

It Matters Not

It matters not what comes to me
    Of sweetest joy or keenest pain.
To work or wait were sweet to me,
    To suffer loss or reap rich gain,
So that He keeps me near His side,
    And His dear name be glorified.

It matters not if life be long,
    Or if my days be short and few;
If rugged steeps and thorny roads,
    Or pleasant vales I journey through,
So that He guides me with His hand,
    And leads me to the promised land.

It matters not. Why should I care?
    Upon His promises I rest:
He crowns me with His tender love
    And robes me in His righteousness.
Come storm or sunshine, night or day,
    I'll sing His praises all the way.

— *Selected*

MY SAVIOUR'S PRAISE

Daily to Thee my soul should raise
   Her notes of love, her notes of joy;
Hourly my heart should sing Thy praise,
   And never cease the blest employ.

Lead me, my God, till at Thy feet
   I cast the crown which Thou wilt give;
Till in the heavenly courts I greet
   The Saviour by whose grace I live.

— Selected

WHY?

Why are you sad when the sky is blue?
Why, when the sun shines brightly for you,
   And the birds are singing, and all the air
   Is sweet with the flowers everywhere?
If life has thorns, it has roses, too.

— Selected

IT MATTERS MUCH

It matters little where I was born,
   Or if my parents were rich or poor;
Whether they shrank at the cold world's scorn
   Or walked in the pride of wealth secure:
But whether I live an honest man,
   And hold my integrity firm in my clutch,
I tell you, my brother, plain as I can,
   It matters much.

It matters little where be my grave,
   If on the land or in the sea;
By purling brook, or 'neath stormy wave,
   It matters little or naught to me;
But whether the angel of death comes down,
   And marks my brow with a loving touch,
As the one who shall wear the victor's crown,
   It matters much.

— *Author unknown*

TRUE TO THYSELF

Choose well thy friends, act well thy part
   In God's mysterious plan,
Remembering that "A foe to God
   Is ne'er true friend to man."

Judge not too harshly when thou see'st
   A fellow mortal stray;
Thou knowest not what temptations have
   Beset him on the way.

Be true to God, true to thyself,
   True to thy fellow man;
So shall life's joys be thine —
   Well spent in fleeting span.

— Selected

LOVING WORDS

Loving words will cost but little,
   Journeying up the hill of life,
But they make the weak and weary
   Stronger, braver for the strife.
Do you count them only trifles?
   What to earth are sun and rain?
Never was a kind word wasted,
   Never one was said in vain.

When the cares of life are many,
   And its burdens heavy grow
For the ones who walk beside you,
   If you love them, tell them so.
What you count of little value,
   Has an almost magic power,
And beneath their cheering sunshine
   Hearts will blossom like a flower.

So, as up life's hill we journey,
   Let us scatter all the way
Kindly words, to be as sunshine
   In the dark and cloudy day.
Grudge no loving word, my brother,
   As along through life you go;
To the ones who journey with you,
   If you love them, tell them so.

— Selected

THE BIBLE

Study it carefully,
Think of it prayerfully,
Deep in thy heart let its pure precepts dwell!
Slight not its history,
Ponder its mystery,
None can e'er prize it too fondly or well.

Accept the glad tidings,
The warnings and chidings,
Found in this volume of heavenly lore;
With faith that's unfailing,
And love all prevailing,
Trust in its promises of life evermore.

With fervent devotion,
And thankful emotion,
Hear the blest welcome, respond to its call;
Life's purest oblation,
The heart's adoration,
Give to the Saviour who died for us all.

May this message of love,
From the tribune above,
To all nations and kindreds be given,
Till the ransomed shall raise
Joyous anthems of praise —
Hallelujah! on earth and in heaven!

— *Author unknown*

GATHERED AT THE LAST

'Mid the losses and the gains,
'Mid the pleasures and the pains,
'Mid the hopings and the fears,
And the restlessness of years,
We repeat this passage o'er
We believe it more and more —
   Bread upon the waters cast
   Shall be gathered at the last.

Gold and silver, like the sands,
Will keep slipping through our hands;
Jewels, gleaming like a spark,
Will be hidden in the dark;
Sun and moon and stars will pale,
But these words will never fail —
   Bread upon the waters cast
   Shall be gathered at the last.

Soon like dust, to you and me,
Will our earthly treasure be;
But the loving word and deed
To a soul in bitterest need,
They will not forgotten be,
They will live eternally —
   Bread upon the waters cast
   Shall be gathered at the last.

Fast the moments slip away,
Soon our mortal powers decay,
Low and lower sinks the sun,
What we do must soon be done;
Then what rapture if we hear
Thousand voices ringing clear —
   Bread upon the waters cast
   Shall be gathered at the last.

— Selected

33

What I Know

I know the summer's day is sweet;
  I know that love is sweeter still;
I know that bliss is ne'er complete;
  I know of no perpetual ill.
I know that life has many sides,
  That some things here seem hardly meet;
I know that baseness often rides,
  While virtue walks with weary feet;
Yet often want and wealth, I know,
  But for each other's mask have stood;
And men, I know, where'er we go,
  Are mostly happy when they're good.
I know that life, on the whole,
  Is well worth all we have to give;
And that the grander is the goal,
  So much the grander 'tis to live.
I know that death is very nigh,
  That evil shrinks before his breath;
That only goodness gives "good-by"
  A rainbow in the cloud of death.

— Selected

Two Things to Learn

Learn to give, and thou shalt bind
  Countless treasures to thy breast;
Learn to love, and thou shalt find
  Only those who love are blest.

— Selected

WATCH YOUR WORDS

Keep a watch on your words, my children,
    For words are wonderful things;
They are sweet, like the bees' fresh honey;
    Like bees, they have terrible stings;
They can bless like the warm glad sunshine
    And brighten the lonely life;
They can cut in the strife of anger
    Like an open, two-edged knife.

Let them pass through your lips unchallenged,
    If their errand be true and kind —
If they come to support the weary,
    To comfort and help the blind.
If a bitter, revengeful spirit
    Prompt the words, let them be unsaid;
They may flash through the brain like lightning,
    Or fall on the heart like lead.

Keep them back, if they're cold and cruel,
    Under bar, and lock, and seal;
The wounds they make, my children,
    Are always slow to heal.
May Christ guard your lips, and ever,
    From the time of your early youth,
May the words you daily utter
    Be the words of the beautiful truth.

                                — *Selected*

THE TEST OF A HERO

It's easy to fight in the cause of the right
    When it's surely, steadily winning;
To nobly stand with a gallant band
    While plaudits loud are dinning;
For nothing inspires and fans the fires
    Of our noblest best endeavor,
Like knowing success will crown our best
    And glory be ours forever.

But to stand with the few and yet be true
    To a seemingly losing cause;
To fight for the right with all our might,
    With never a sound of applause;
To stand like a brave in the face of a grave,
    O'erhung with the cloud of defeat,
This, this is the test of a hero, the best,
    A hero we seldom meet.

— Author unknown

JUST FOR TODAY

Lord, for tomorrow and its needs,
    I do not pray;
Keep me from stain of sin
    Just for today.

Let me both diligently work
    And duly pray;
Let me be kind in word and deed
    Just for today.

Let me be slow to do my will —
    Prompt to obey;
Help me to sacrifice myself
    Just for today.

Let me no wrong or idle word
    Unthinking say;
Set thou a seal upon my lips
    Just for today.

So, for tomorrow and its needs
    I do not pray;
But keep me, guide me, hold me, Lord,
    Just for today.

— *Sybil F. Partridge*

STEP BY STEP

Child of my love, fear not the unknown tomorrow,
 Dread not the new demand life makes of thee;
Thy ignorance doth hold no cause for sorrow,
 Since what thou knowest not is known to Me.

Thou canst not see today the hidden meaning
 Of My command, but thou the light shall gain.
Walk on in faith, upon My promise leaning,
 And as thou goest all shall be made plain.

One step thou seest — then go forward boldly;
 One step is far enough for faith to see;
Take that, and thy next duty shall be told thee,
 For step by step thy Lord is leading thee.

Stand not in fear, thy adversaries counting;
 Dare every peril; scorn to disobey;
Thou shalt march on, all obstacles surmounting,
 For I, the Strong, will open up the way.

Wherefore go gladly to the task assigned thee;
 Having My promise, needing nothing more
Than just to know, where'er the future find thee,
 In all thy journeying I go before.

— Author unknown

PERSONAL BATTLES

There's many a battle fought daily
  The world knows nothing about.
There's many a brave young soldier
  Whose strength puts a legion to rout,
And he who fights sin single-handed
  Is more of a hero, I say,
Than he who leads soldiers to battle
  And conquers by arms in the fray.

— Author unknown

BY FAITH, NOT BY SIGHT

God would never send you the darkness
If He felt you could bear the light;
But you would not cling to His guiding hand
If the way were always bright;
And you would not care to walk by faith
Could you always walk by sight.

— Selected

GOD'S PROMISE

Has a sorrow come upon you
   That no other soul can share?
Does the burden seem too heavy
   For your aching heart to bear?
There is One whose love can comfort
   If you'll trust Him with your load,
There's a Burden-Bearer ready,
   If you'll give Him an abode;
Lo! the precious promise reaches
   To the depth of human woe,
That however deep the waters
   They shall never overflow!

Does your flesh seem worn and weary
   And your spirits grow depressed?
Does life's tempest sweep upon you
   Like a storm on ocean's breast?
Let me whisper there's a haven
   Open for the weary bird,
And a refuge for the tempted
   In the promise of God's Word;
Let the standard of His Spirit
   E'er be raised against the foe —
Then however deep the waters,
   They shall never overflow.

Do you ever grow discouraged
　　As you journey on your way?
Does there seem to be more darkness
　　Than there is of sunny day?
Ah, 'tis hard to learn the lesson
　　As you pass beneath the rod,
That the shadow and the sunshine
　　Are alike the will of God.
Let me speak a word of promise
　　Like the promise in the bow —
That however deep the waters
　　They shall never overflow.

When the sands of life are ebbing,
　　And you near the Jordan's shore,
When you see the billows rising
　　And you hear the waters roar,
Just reach out your hand to Jesus
　　In His tender bosom hide.
Then 'twill only be a moment
　　Till you reach the other side;
Then indeed the fullest meaning
　　Of His promise you shall know —
When thou passest through the waters
　　They shall never overflow.

— Selected

I Can Do All Things

I can do all things! I can do all things!
    You ask how this may be?
Here is my answer: "I can do all things
    Thro' Christ which strength'neth me."

This is not boasting; that were excluded;
    To Him all praise must be;
His strength made perfect in utter weakness,
    He gives the victory.

I can do nothing — without Him, nothing;
    Too oft' I thus have striv'n;
All vain and fruitless my best endeavor,
    Unless His strength be giv'n.

Ah, yes! without Him, I faint and languish —
    A withered branch would be;
In Him abiding, "I can do all things
    Thro' Christ which strength'neth me."

"Most gladly, therefore, I rather, glory
    In my infirmities,"
For when I'm weakest, then am I strongest,
    Not in my strength — but His.

                    — *T. O. Chisholm*

Being Pleasant

It's easy enough to be pleasant
   When life goes on like a song,
But the man worth while
Is the man who can smile
   When everything goes dead wrong.

— Author unknown

Christ's Message

Christ has no hands but our hands
To do His work today;
He has no feet but our feet
To lead men in His way.

He has no tongue but our tongues
To tell men how He died;
He has no help but our help
To lead men to His side.

We are the Lord's only message
The careless world will read;
We are the sinner's Gospel,
We are the scoffer's creed.

We are the Lord's last message,
Written in deed and word.
What if the type be crooked?
What if the print be blurred?

— Author unknown

I Am Debtor

When this passing world is done,
When has sunk yon glaring sun,
When we stand with Christ in glory,
Looking o'er life's finished story;
Then, Lord, shall I fully know —
Not till then — how much I owe.

When I stand before the throne,
Dressed in beauty not my own;
When I see Thee as thou art,
Love Thee with unsinning heart;
Then, Lord, shall I fully know —
Not till then — how much I owe.

Chosen not for good in me,
Wakened up from wrath to flee;
Hidden in the Saviour's side,
By the Spirit sanctified;
Teach me, Lord, on earth to show,
By my love, how much I owe.

— *Robert Murray M'Cheyne*

Mercy Followed Me

Minutes and mercies multiplied
Have made up all my days;
Minutes came quick, but mercies were
More fleet and free than they.

— *J. Mason*

VICE

In some gay hour vice steals into the breast;
Perchance she wears some softer virtue's vest;
By unperceived degrees she tempts to stray,
Till far from virtue's path she leads the feet away.

— *S. T. Coleridge*

LEAVE ALL TO GOD

Leave God to order all thy ways,
And hope in Him, whate'er betide;
Thou'lt find Him in the evil days
Thine all-sufficient strength and guide.

— *Selected*

Not Your Own

"Not your own!" but His ye are
  Who hath paid a price untold
For your life, exceeding far
  All earth's store of gems and gold.

With the precious blood of Christ,
Ransom treasure all unpriced,
Full redemption is secured,
Full salvation is assured.

"Not your own!" but His by right;
  His peculiar treasure now,
Fair and precious in His sight,
  Purchased jewels for His brow.

He will keep what thus He sought,
Safely guard the dearly bought,
Cherish that which He did choose,
Always love and never lose.

"Not your own!" but His, the King;
  His, the Lord of earth and sky;
His to Whom archangels bring
  Homage deep and praises high.

What can royal birth bestow
Or the proudest titles know?
Can such dignity be known
As the glorious name, "His own"?

"Not your own!" to Him ye owe
   All your life and all your love;
Live, that ye His praises may show,
   Who is yet all praise above.

Every day and every hour,
Every gift and every power
Consecrate to Him alone,
Who hath claimed you for His own.

Teach us, Master, how to give
   All we have and are to Thee;
Grant us, Saviour, while we live,
   Wholly, only Thine to be,

Henceforth be our calling high,
Thee to serve and glorify;
Ours no longer, but Thine own,
Thine forever, Thine alone!

— *Frances Ridley Havergal*

THE VICTORY OF FAITH

Though the fig tree shall not blossom
  And the vines are bare,
Though the fatness of the olive
  May not be my share
Though the fields are not in verdure,
  And the flocks are dead —
Yet the God of my salvation
  Doth anoint my head.

God, the God of my salvation,
  Bears me on His wing,
Far above to His high places,
  There with Him to sing;
He will make my feet like hind's feet,
  Guide my feet to tread
Spheres of light and life abounding,
  Where His love is shed.

O "Chief Singer," tune my Spirit
  Into perfect praise,
For Thy worship, for Thine honor,
  Songs my heart would raise;
Touch the instrument of ten strings,
  Vibrate every key,
Swell the chord, awaken music
  In my soul for Thee.

— S. C. M. A.

Thou Paschal Lamb, appointed
   By God the Father's love;
That we, through His anointed
   Might all His mercy prove:
Through Thee we have salvation,
   Life, pardon, peace obtained;
And praise with adoration,
   The Lamb for sinners slain.

Freedom from condemnation
   Could only come by Thee;
Through Thy humiliation
   And sufferings on the tree.
Thy weight of sorrow bearing
   From Satan, man, and God,
And love to us declaring
   Through Thine atoning blood.

We praise Thee, Holy Saviour,
   That Thou didst suffer thus,
And in Thy loving favor
   Endure the curse for us.
Through everlasting ages
   All glory be to Thee;
While this, each heart engages,
   Thy love on Calvary.

We wait for Thine appearing
   To chase the night away,
The welcome summons hearing
   To call us hence away.
Thy saints will then in glory
   Redeeming love proclaim,
While they rejoice before Thee
   That "Worthy is the Lamb."

— Selected

Thanks, Lord Jesus

Christ, the Life of all the living,
   Christ, the Death of death, our foe,
Who Thyself for me once giving
   To the darkest depths of woe,
Patiently didst yield Thy breath
But to save my soul from death;
Thousand, thousand thanks shall be
O Lord Jesus, unto Thee.

Thou didst bear the smiting only
   That it might not fall on me;
Stoodest falsely charged and lonely,
   That I might be safe and free;
Comfortless that I might know
Comfort from Thy boundless woe;
Thousand, thousand thanks shall be,
O Lord Jesus, unto Thee.

— Ernst C. Homberg
Trans. by Catherine Winkworth

ALL TO THEE

All that we *were* — our sins, our guilt,
  Our death — was all our own
All that we *are* we owe to Thee,
  Thou God of grace alone.

Thy mercy found us in our sins,
  And gave us to believe;
Then, in believing, peace we found;
  And in Christ we live.

All that we are, as saints on earth,
  All that we hope to be
When Jesus comes and glory dawns,
  We owe it all to Thee.

— H. Bonar

HARVEST-TIME

He that goeth forth with weeping,
   Bearing precious seed in love,
Never tiring, never sleeping,
   Findeth mercy from above:
Soft descend the dews of heaven
   Bright the rays celestial shine;
Precious fruits will thus be given
   Through an influence all divine.

Sow thy seed; be never weary;
   Let no fears thy soul annoy;
Be the prospect ne'er so dreary,
   Thou shalt reap the fruits of joy.
Lo! the scene of verdure brightening,
   See the rising grain appear:
Look again; the fields are whitening.
   For the harvest-time is near.

                             — *Thomas Hastings*

Lord, Give Me Faith

Lord, give me faith to live from day to day,
With tranquil heart to do my simple part,
And with my hand in Thine just go Thy way;
Lord, give me faith to leave it all to Thee.
The future is Thy gift; I would not lift
The veil Thy love has flung 'twixt it and me.

— John Oxenham

Ready

Ready to go, ready to stay,
Ready my place to fill;
Ready for service, lowly or great,
Ready to do His will.

— Selected

HEART'S JOURNEY

O Thou who dost direct my feet
　　To right or left, where pathways part,
Wilt Thou not, faithful Paraclete,
　　Direct the journeyings of my heart?

Into the love of God, I pray,
　　Deeper and deeper let me press;
Exploring all along the way
　　Its secret strength and tenderness.

Into the steadfastness of One
　　Who patiently endured the cross,
Of Him who, though He were a Son,
　　Came to His crown through bitter loss.

This is the road of my desire —
　　Learning to love as God loves me;
Ready to pass through flood or fire
　　With Christ's unwearying constancy.

— Author unknown

No Change in Him

Whate'er my change, in Him no change is seen,
A glorious sun, that wanes not, nor declines,
Above the clouds and storms He walks serene,
And sweetly on His people's darkness shines.
All may depart — I fret not, nor repine,
While I my Saviour's am, while He is mine.

He stays me falling, lifts me up when down;
Reclaims me wandering, guards from every foe;
Plants on my worthless brow the victor's crown
Which, in return, before His feet I throw,
Grieved that I cannot better grace His shrine,
Who deigns to own me His, as He is mine.

— *A. C. Gaebelein*

JESUS, MY SIN-BEARER

I lay my sins on Jesus,
　The spotless Lamb of God;
He bears them all, and frees us
　From the accursed load.
I bring my guilt to Jesus,
　To wash my crimson stains
White in His blood most precious,
　Till not a spot remains.

I lay my wants on Jesus;
　All fullness dwells in Him;
He heals all my diseases,
　He doth my soul redeem.
I lay my griefs on Jesus,
　My burdens and my cares;
He from them all releases,
　He all my sorrows shares.

I long to be like Jesus,
　Meek, loving, lowly, mild;
I long to be, like Jesus,
　The Father's Holy Child.
I long to be with Jesus,
　Amid the heavenly throng,
To sing with saints His praises,
　To learn the angel's song.

— *H. Bonar*

The Time Is Short

If thou wouldst work for God, it must be now;
If thou wouldst win the garland for thy brow,
      Redeem the time.

      With His reward
He comes. He tarries not; His day is near;
When men least look for Him; will He be here;
      Prepare for Him!

— H. Bonar

Faith's Effect

Faith came singing into my room:
    Its other guests took flight.
Fear and anxiety, grief and gloom,
    Sped out into the night;
And I wondered how such peace could be —
    Faith said gently, "Don't you see?
They really could not live with me!"

— Selected

DON'T JUDGE TOO HARD

Pray don't find fault with the man who limps,
　　Or stumbles along the road,
Unless you have worn the shoes he wears
　　Or struggled beneath his load.
There may be tacks in his shoes that hurt,
　　Though hidden from view,
Or the burden he bears, placed on your back,
　　Might cause you to stumble, too.

Don't sneer at the man who's down today,
　　Unless you have felt the blow
That caused his fall, or felt the shame
　　That only the fallen know.
You may be strong, but still the blows
　　That were his, if dealt on you,
In the selfsame way, at the selfsame time,
　　Might cause you to stagger, too.

Don't be too harsh with the man who sins
　　Or pelt him with words or stones,
Unless you are sure, yea, doubly sure,
　　That you have no sins of your own.
For you know perhaps, if the tempter's voice
　　Should whisper as soft to you
As it did to him when he went astray,
　　'Twould cause you to falter, too.

— Selected

OUR SHEPHERD

Our Shepherd is the Lord,
   The living Lord who died;
With all His fulness can afford
   We are supplied.
He richly feeds our souls
   With blessings from above;
And leads us where the river rolls
   Of endless love.

When faith and hope shall cease,
   And love abide alone,
Then shall we see Him face to face,
   And know as known;
Still shall we lift our voice,
   His praise our song shall be;
And we shall in His love rejoice
   Who set us free.

— Beaumont

None Other Name

None other Lamb, none other Name,
  None other Hope in heaven or earth or sea,
None other Hiding-place from guilt and shame,
  None beside Thee.

My faith burns low, my hope burns low;
  Only my heart's desire cries out in me
By the deep thunder of its want and woe,
  Cries out to Thee.

Lord, Thou art Life, though I be dead,
  Love's Fire Thou art, however cold I be:
Nor heaven have I, nor place to lay my head
  Nor home but Thee.

— Christina Rossetti

God's Plans

Some time when all life's lessons have been learned,
  And sun and stars forevermore have set,
The things which our weak judgment here has spurned,
  The things o'er which we grieve with lashes wet,
Will flash before us clear in life's dark night,
  As stars shine most in deepest tints of blue;
And we shall see how all God's plans are right,
  And what most seemed reproof was love most true.

— Selected

ONLY WAIT

Oft there comes a gentle whisper o'er me stealing
    When my trials and my burdens seem too great;
Like the sweet-voiced bells of evening softly pealing,
    It is saying to my spirit — "Only wait."

When I cannot understand my Father's leading,
    And it seems but hard and cruel fate,
Still I hear that gentle whisper ever pleading,
    "God is working, God is faithful — Only wait."

When the promise seems to linger, long delaying,
    And I tremble lest perhaps it comes too late,
Still I hear that sweet-voiced angel saying,
    "Though it tarry, it is coming — Only wait."

When I see the wicked prosper in their sinning,
    And the righteous pressed by many a cruel strait,
I remember this is only the beginning,
    And I whisper to my spirit — "Only wait."

O how little soon will seem my hardest sorrow,
    And how trifling is our present brief estate:
Could we see it in the light of heaven's tomorrow,
    O how easy it would be for us to wait.

— Selected

61

To Be With Jesus There

Ah! who upon earth can conceive
    The bliss that with Jesus we'll share?
Or who this dark world would not leave,
    And earnestly long to be there?
There Christ is the light and the sun,
    His glories unhinderedly shine;
Already our joy is begun,
    Our rest is the glory divine.

'Tis good, at His word, to be here,
    Yet better e'en now to be gone;
And there in His presence appear,
    And rest where He rests on the throne.
Yet, ah! what great joy 'twill afford,
    When Him we shall see in the air;
And enter the joy of the Lord,
    For ever to be with Him there.

— Charles Wesley

THE UNSEEN LINE

There is a line, by us unseen
That crosses every path,
The hidden boundary between
God's patience and His wrath.

— *Selected*

HE KNOWS

Trust Him, He knows our troubled state;
He knows each winding of the road;
Let us sit calmly down and wait;
"Be still and know that I am God."

— *Selected*

JESUS CAME

Jesus came! — and came for me —
Simple words! and yet expressing
Depths of holy mystery,
Depths of wondrous love and blessing.
Holy Spirit, make me see
All His coming means for me;
Take the things of Christ, I pray,
Show them to my heart today.

— *Frances Ridley Havergal*

OPEN MY EYES

Open my eyes, that I may see
This one and that one needing Thee;
Hearts that are dumb, unsatisfied;
Lives that are dark, for whom Christ died.
Open my eyes in sympathy
Clear into man's deep soul to see;
Wise with Thy wisdom to discern,
And with Thy heart of love to yearn.
Open my eyes in power, I pray,
Give me the strength to speak today,
Someone to bring, dear Lord, to Thee;
Use me, O Lord, use even me.

— *Betty Scott Stam*

GLAD SURPRISE

Where'er a noble deed is wrought,
Where'er is spoken a noble thought,
Our hearts in glad surprise
To higher levels rise.

— *Selected*

TAKE COURAGE

Courage, brother! do not stumble,
  Though thy path be dark as night;
There's a star to guide the humble:
  Trust in God and do the right.
Let the road be rough and dreary,
  And its end far out of sight,
Foot it bravely; strong or weary,
  Trust in God and do the right.

Perish policy and cunning,
  Perish all that fears the light!
Whether losing, whether winning,
  Trust in God and do the right.
Some will hate thee, some will love thee,
  Some will flatter, some will slight;
Cease from man, and look above thee;
  Trust in God and do the right.

— *N. Macleod*

A Missionary's Question

There are times when the enemy seems to prevail
 And faintness creeps over the heart,

When courage and confidence quiver and quail
 At the glance of his fiery dart.

There are times when exhausted, we can but stand still,
 When the sword-arm hangs nerveless and numb,

Oh, then to the soul comes a whisper so chill:
 "Are they weary of praying at home?"

— *Selected*

Speak to Him

Speak to Him, then, for He heareth,
 And spirit with spirit doth meet.
Closer is He than breathing,
 Nearer than hands and feet.

— *Selected*

A PRAYER

Like the publican of old,
I can only urge the plea,
"Lord, be merciful to me!"
Nothing of desert I claim
Unto me belongeth shame.

Let the lowliest task be mine,
Grateful, so the work be Thine;
Let me find the humblest place
In the shadow of Thy grace:
Blest to me were any spot
Where temptation whispers not.
If there be some weaker one,
Give me strength to help him on;
If a blinder soul there be,
Let me guide him nearer Thee.
Make my mortal dreams come true
With the work I fain would do;
Clothe with life the weak intent,
Let me be the thing I meant;
Let me find in Thy employ
Peace that dearer is than joy;
Out of self to love be led
And to heaven acclimated,
Until all things sweet and good
Seem my natural habitude.

— *John Greenleaf Whittier*

Nothing Without Love

Had I the tongues of Greeks and Jews,
And nobler speech than angels use;
If love be absent, I am found
Like tinkling brass, an empty sound.

Were I inspired to preach, and tell
All that is done in heaven and hell;
Or could my faith the world remove,
Still — I am nothing without love.

Should I distribute all my store
To feed the bowels of the poor;
Or give my body to the flame,
To gain a martyr's glorious name;

If love to God and love to men
Be absent — all my hopes are vain;
Nor tongues, nor gifts, nor fiery zeal,
The works of love can e'er fulfill.

— Isaac Watts

Jesus Paid It All

The trembling sinner feareth
That God can ne'er forget;
But one full payment cleareth
His memory of all debt.

When naught beside could ease us
Or set our souls at large,
Thy holy work, Lord Jesus,
Secured a full discharge.

— *Selected*

Speak to Us

Speak to us, Lord, until our hearts are melted,
To share in Thy compassion for the lost:
Till our souls throb with burning intercession,
That they shall know Thy name, whate'er the cost.

Speak to us, Lord, till shamed by Thy great giving,
Our hands unclasp to set our treasures free;
Our wills, our love, our dear ones, our possessions,
All gladly yielded, gracious Lord, to Thee.

— *Author unknown*

RISE UP, O MEN OF GOD

Rise up, O men of God!
Have done with lesser things;
Give heart and soul and mind and strength
To serve the King of kings.

Rise up, O men of God!
His kingdom tarries long;
Bring in the day of brotherhood,
And end the night of wrong.

Rise up, O men of God!
The Church for you doth wait;
Her strength shall make your spirit strong,
Her service make you great.

Lift high the cross of Christ!
Tread where His feet have trod;
As brothers of the Son of Man
Rise up, O men of God!

— *William P. Merrill*
Used by permission of *The
Presbyterian Outlook*, Richmond, Va.

THE TONGUE

"The boneless tongue, so small and weak,
Can crush and kill," declared the Greek.
"The tongue destroys a greater horde,"
The Turk asserts, "than does the sword."
The Persian proverb wisely saith,
"A lengthy tongue, an early death."
Or sometimes takes this form instead:
"Don't let your tongue cut off your head."
"The tongue can speak a word whose speed,"
Says the Chinese, "outstrips the steed."
While Arab sages this impart:
"The tongue's great storehouse is the heart."
From Hebrew with the maxim sprung:
"Though feet should slip, ne'er let the tongue."
The sacred writer crowns the whole:
"Who keeps his tongue doth keep his soul."

— *Selected*

LORD OF THE HARVEST

Sing to the Lord of the harvest,
  Sing songs of love and praise;
With joyful hearts and voices
  Your hallelujahs raise:
By Him the rolling seasons
  In fruitful order move,
Sing to the Lord of harvest
  A song of happy love.

By Him the clouds drop fatness,
  The deserts bloom and spring.
The hills leap up in gladness,
  The valleys laugh and sing:
He filleth with His fulness
  All things with large increase;
He crowns the year with goodness,
  With plenty and with peace.

Heap on His sacred altar
  The gifts His goodness gave,
The golden sheaves of harvest,
  The souls He died to save:
Your hearts lay down before Him
  When at His feet ye fall,
And with your lives adore Him
  Who gave His life for all.

To God the gracious Father,
  Who made us "very good";
To Christ who, when we wandered,
  Restored us with His blood;
And to the Holy Spirit,
  Who doth upon us pour
His blessed dews and sunshine
  Be praise for evermore.

— *John S. B. Monsell*

My Father's World

This is my Father's world,
Oh, let me ne'er forget
That though the wrong seems oft so strong,
God is the ruler yet.
This is my Father's world:
The battle is not done;
Jesus who died shall be satisfied,
And earth and heaven be one.

— Maltbie D. Babcock

Forget It

If you see a tall fellow ahead of a crowd,
A leader of men, marching fearless and proud,
And you know of a tale whose mere telling aloud
Would cause that proud head to in anguish be bowed,
It's a pretty good thing to forget it.

— Selected

What to Build On

Build on resolve, and not upon regret,
    The structure of thy future. Do not grope
Among the shadows of old sins; but let
    Thine own soul's light shine on the path of hope.
And dissipate the darkness! Waste not tears
    Upon the blackened record of past years!
But turn to live; and smile, oh, smile to see
    The fair white pages that remain to thee.

— Selected

I Love Thee

O God, I love Thee; not that my poor love
May win me entrance to Thy heaven above,
Nor yet that strangers to Thy love must know
The bitterness of everlasting woe.

How can I choose but love Thee, God's dear Son!
O Jesus, loveliest and most loving One?
Were there no heaven to gain, no hell to flee,
For what Thou art alone I must love Thee.

Not for the hope of glory or reward,
But even as Thyself has loved me, Lord,
I love Thee, and will love Thee and adore,
Who art my King, my God forevermore.

— An old hymn

A Missionary Cry

A hundred thousand souls a day
Are passing one by one away,
    In Christless guilt and gloom,
Without one ray of hope or light,
With future dark as endless night,
    They're passing to their doom.

O Holy Ghost, Thy people move,
Baptize their hearts with faith and love,
    And consecrate their gold;
At Jesus' feet their millions pour,
And all their ranks unite once more,
    As in the days of old.

Armies of prayer your promise claim,
Prove the full power of Jesus' name,
    And take the victory.
Your conquering Captain leads you on,
The glorious fight may still be won,
    This very century.

The Master's coming draweth near,
The Son of man will soon appear,
    His kingdom is at hand.
But ere that glorious day can be,
The Gospel of the Kingdom we
    Must preach in every land.

They're passing, passing fast away,
A hundred thousand souls a day,
    In Christless guilt and gloom,
O Church of Christ what wilt thou say
When in that awful judgment day
    They charge thee with their doom!

            — A. B. Simpson

A TREASURE

There is a treasure
Rich beyond measure,
Offered to mortals today;
Some folk despise it,
Some criticize it,
Some would explain it away.

Some never read it,
Some never heed it,
Some say it's long had its day;
Some people prize it,
And he who tries it,
Finds it his comfort and stay.

God gave this treasure
Rich beyond measure —
His Word, we call it today.
Let us believe it,
Gladly receive it,
Read, mark and learn to obey.

— Author unknown

PRAISE

Immortal, invisible,
God only wise
In light inaccessible,
Hid from our eyes.
Most blessed, most glorious,
The Ancient of Days,
Almighty, victorious.
Thy great Name we praise.

— Walter Chalmers Smith

A BACKSLIDER'S PRAYER

O Jesus, full of truth and grace,
More full of grace than I of sin,
Yet once again I seek Thy face;
Open Thine arms and take me in,
And freely my backsliding heal,
And love the faithless sinner still.

Thou know'st the way to bring me back,
My fallen spirit to restore:
O! for Thy truth and mercy's sake,
Forgive, and bid me sin no more;
The ruins of my soul repair,
And make my heart a house of prayer.

— Author unknown

Homes

So long as there are homes to which men turn
At close of day;
So long as there are homes where children are,
Where mothers stay —
If love and truth and Christian faith be found
Across those sills —
The Church of Christ can overcome
The gravest ills.

So long as there are homes where fires burn
And where there is bread;
So long as there are homes where Christ can dwell
And prayers are said;
Although men falter through the dark —
And nations grope —
With God Himself inside these loving homes —
We have sure hope.

— Selected

The Weaver

My life is but a weaving
  Between my Lord and me;
I cannot choose the colors;
  He worketh steadily.

Ofttimes He weaveth sorrow,
  And I, in foolish pride,
Forget He sees the upper,
  And I the under side.

Not till the loom is silent
  And the shuttles cease to fly
Shall God unroll the canvas,
  And explain the reason why

The dark threads are as needful
  In the Weaver's skillful hand
As the threads of gold and silver
  In the pattern He has planned.

— Christian Index

My Times Are in Thy Hands

I'm glad my times are in Thy hands:
    It is so sweet to know
That everything by Thee is planned
    For me where'er I go;
The hand that holds the ocean's depths
    Can hold my small affairs;
The hand that guides the universe
    Can carry all my cares.

Thou seest all that's coming, Lord,
    The pleasure and the pain;
And Thou art shaping all for me
    And my eternal gain.
Thy hand is one of love and power,
    So gentle yet so strong,
It surely can control all things
    Which unto me belong.

I'm glad I cannot shape my way,
    I'd rather have Thy will;
I'm glad the ordering is not mine
    I'd rather have Thy will;
I do not know the future, and
    I would not if I might,
For faith to me is better far
    Than faulty human sight.

My times are in Thy hands, O Lord,
    'Tis restful it is so;
And as I tread an untried way,
    'Tis quieting to know
That my dear Father up in heaven
    Doth understand my case,
So I can safely trust to Him
    All till I see His face.

— *Selected*

O LOVE DIVINE

O Love divine, Thou vast abyss!
Our sins are swallowed up in Thee,
Covered is our unrighteousness;
From condemnation we are free:
In Jesus' blood our hearts can trace
The boundless riches of Thy grace.

Fixed on this ground must we remain;
Though heart may fail and flesh decay,
This anchor shall our souls sustain;
When earth and heaven shall pass away,
Mercy's full worth we then shall prove —
Loved with an everlasting love.

— *J. A. Rothe*

AFTER

Light after darkness, gain after loss,
Strength after weakness, crown after cross;
Sweet after bitter, hope after fears,
Home after wandering, praise after tears.

— *Author unknown*

A Song of Praise

We praise Thee, we bless Thee, our Saviour divine,
All power and dominion for ever be Thine!
We sing of Thy mercy with joyful acclaim,
For Thou hast redeemed us: all praise to Thy name!

All honour and praise to Thine excellent name,
Thy love is unchanging — forever the same!
We bless and adore Thee, O Saviour and King;
With joy and thanksgiving Thy praises we sing!

The strength of the hills and the depths of the sea,
The earth and its fulness, belong unto Thee;
And yet to the lowly Thou bendest Thine ear,
So ready their humble petitions to hear.

Thine infinite goodness our tongues shall employ,
Thou givest us richly all things to enjoy;
We'll follow Thy footsteps, we'll rest in Thy love,
And soon we shall praise Thee in mansions above!

— Fanny J. Crosby

The Ten Commandments in Verse

Thou shalt have no other gods but Me;
Before no idol bow the knee;
Take not the Name of God in vain;
Nor dare the Sabbath day profane;
Give both thy parents honor due;
Take heed that thou no murder do;
Abstain from words and deeds unclean;
Nor steal, though thou be poor and mean;
Nor make a willful lie, nor love it;
What is thy neighbor's, dare not covet.

— Now

Have You Counted the Cost?

You may barter your hope of eternity's morn,
    For a moment of joy at the most,
For the glitter of sin and the things it will win,
    Have you counted the cost, have you counted the cost?

— A. J. Hodge

GOD'S MERCY

There's a wideness in God's mercy
Like the wideness of the sea;
There's a kindness in His justice
Which is more than liberty.

There is welcome for the sinner,
And more graces for the good;
There is mercy with the Saviour;
There is healing in His blood.

For the love of God is broader
Than the measure of man's mind.
And the heart of the Eternal
Is most wonderfully kind.

If our love were but more simple,
We should take Him at His Word,
And our lives would be more holy
In the glory of the Lord.

— *Frederick W. Faber*

KNOWING GOD'S LOVE

I have heard it passeth knowledge,
  I believe what God hath said;
But the test is, do I prove it
  As my daily path I tread?
Is it merely that I think it,
  And accept what others say?
Does it fill my heart with singing,
  Is it in me day by day?

What is knowledge worth that's buried
  Like a jewel in the earth?
If we know God's love, our knowledge
  Must live in us — giving birth
To a love that feels for others,
  Looks upon them from God's side;
Lord, just keep me in that knowledge,
  Let me in Thy love abide!

— *Selected*

If Jesus Christ Is

If Jesus Christ is a man,
And only a man, I say
That of all mankind I cleave to Him,
And to Him I will cleave alway.

If Jesus Christ is a God,
And the only God, I swear
I will follow Him through heaven and hell,
The earth, the sea and the air.

— Richard Watson Gilder

My King's Business

I am a stranger here, within a foreign land;
   My home is far away, upon a golden strand;
Ambassador to be of realms beyond the sea,
   I'm here on business for my King.

My home is brighter far than Sharon's rosy plain,
   Eternal life and joy throughout its vast domain;
My Sov'reign bids me tell how mortals there may dwell,
   And that's my business for my King.

— E. T. Cassel

CHRIST'S PLAN FOR ME

When I stand at the judgment seat of Christ,
    And He shows His plan for me —
The plan of my life as it might have been
    Had He had His way, and I see
How I blocked Him there, and I checked Him here
    And I would not yield my will —
Will there be grief in my Saviour's eyes,
    Grief, though He loves me still?

He would have me rich, and I stand there poor,
    Stripped of all but His grace,
While memory runs like a hunted thing
    Down the path I cannot retrace!
Then my desolate heart will well-nigh break
    With the tears I cannot shed;
I will cover my face with my empty hands,
    I will bow my uncrowned head.

Oh, Lord of the years that are left to me,
    I give them to Thy hand;
Take me, and break me, mould me to
    The pattern that Thou hast planned.

                                    — *Selected*

The Lord Is My Shepherd

The Lord has e'er my Shepherd been, my keeper
  in the night;
'Tis He who leads me step by step, who guides
  me in the light,
When I am lost and darkness falls, when steep
  the rocky way,
'Tis Christ, the Shepherd of my Soul, who seeks
  me when I stray.

I shall not want, for He is mine, He satisfies
  each plea,
And though I through the valley walk, I know
  He's there with me.
He leadeth me, O blessed thought, beside the
  waters still,
The wondrous peace of knowing Him, my hungry
  soul doth fill.
I shall not fear though waters deep, through
  valleys I must roam,
For Christ my Shepherd e'er shall be, until He
  leads me home.

— *Connie Calenberg*

A NOBLE AMBITION

Quiet, Lord, my froward heart;
Make me teachable and mild,
Upright, simple, free from art;
Make me as a weaned child;
From distrust and envy free,
Pleased with all that pleases Thee.

— John Newton

ON GIVING

"What! Giving again?" I asked in dismay,
"And must I keep giving and giving away?"
"Oh, no," said the angel, piercing me through,
"Just give till the Father stops giving to you."

— Selected

Psalm 103

O bless the Lord, my soul;
   Let all within me join,
And aid my tongue to bless His Name,
   Whose favors are divine.
O bless the Lord, my soul,
   Nor let His mercies lie
Forgotten in unthankfulness,
   And without praises die.

'Tis He forgives thy sins,
   'Tis He relieves thy pain,
'Tis He that heals thy sicknesses,
   And makes thee young again.
He crowns thy life with love,
   When ransomed from the grave;
He that redeemed my soul from hell
   Hath sovereign power to save.

He fills the poor with good;
   He gives the sufferers rest:
The Lord hath judgments for the proud,
   And justice for the oppressed.
His wondrous works and ways
   He made by Moses known;
But sent the world His truth and grace
   By His beloved Son.

— Isaac Watts

THOU WHO CAMEST FROM ABOVE

O Thou, who camest from above,
The pure celestial fire to impart,
Kindle a flame of sacred love
On the mean altar of my heart.

There let it for Thy glory burn
With inextinguishable blaze,
And trembling to its source return,
In humble prayer and fervent praise.

Jesus, confirm my heart's desire
To work, and speak, and think for Thee;
Still let me guard the holy fire;
And still stir up Thy gift in me:

Ready for all Thy perfect will,
My acts of faith and love repeat,
Till death Thy endless mercies seal,
And make the sacrifice complete.

— Charles Wesley

WE SEE A LITTLE

We only see a little of the ocean,
    A few miles distance from the rocky shore;
But, oh, out there beyond the eye's horizon
    There's more — there's more!

We only see a little of God's love
    A few rich treasures from His mighty store;
But, oh, out there beyond — beyond the life's horizon,
    There's more — there's more.

— *Author unknown*

DEATH IN LIFE

He always said he would retire
    When he had made a million clear,
And so he toiled into the dusk
    From day to day, from year to year.

At last he put his ledgers up
    And laid his stock reports aside —
But when he started out to live
    He found he had already died!

— *Author unknown*

THE RICHER SACRIFICE

Not all the blood of beasts
   On Jewish altars slain
Could give the guilty conscience peace,
   Or wash away the stain.
But Christ, the heavenly Lamb,
   Takes all our sins away.
A Sacrifice of nobler name
   And richer blood than they.

— Isaac Watts

THE MASTER'S POWER

Lord, I have not strength to serve Thee much,
   The half day's work is all that I can do,
But let Thy mighty, multiplying touch
   Even to me the miracle renew.
Let one word feed five thousand
   And Thy power
Expand to life's results
   One earnest, feeble hour.

— Author unknown

THE LORD'S WAY

I asked the Lord that I might grow
In faith and love and every grace;
Might more of His salvation know,
And seek more earnestly His face.

'Twas He who taught me thus to pray,
And He, I trust, has answered prayer;
But it has been in such a way
As almost drove me to despair.

I hoped that in some favor'd hour
At once He'd answer my request;
And, by His love's constraining power,
Subdue my sins, and give me rest.

Instead of this, He made me feel
The hidden evils of my heart,
And let the angry powers of hell
Assault my soul in every part.

Yea, more, with His own hand He seem'd
Intent to aggravate my woe;
Cross'd all the fair designs I schemed,
Blasted my gourds, and laid them low.

"Lord, why is this?" I trembling cried:
"Wilt Thou pursue Thy worm to death?"
" 'Tis in this way," the Lord replied,
"I answer prayer for grace and faith.

"These inward trials I employ,
From self and pride to set thee free
And break thy schemes of earthly joy,
That thou mayst seek thy all in Me."

— *Author unknown*

The Two Builders

A builder builded a temple,
    He wrought it with grace and skill,
Pillars and groins and arches,
    All fashioned to work his will,
Men said as they saw its beauty,
    "It shall never know decay.
Great is thy skill, O builder,
    Thy fame shall endure for aye."

A teacher builded a temple
    With loving and infinite care,
Planning each arch with patience,
    Laying each stone with prayer.
None praised his unceasing efforts,
    None knew of his wondrous plan,
For the temple the teacher builded
    Was unseen by the eyes of man.

Gone is the builder's temple,
    Crumbled into the dust;
Low lies each stately pillar,
    Food for consuming rust.
But the temple the teacher builded
    Will last while the ages roll,
For that beautiful unseen temple
    Is a child's immortal soul.

— Author unknown

TRIALS AND HAPPINESS

Trials must and will befall,
    But with humble faith to see
Love inscribed upon them all —
    This is happiness for me.

— Author unknown

LOVE BENDS

Love has a hem to its garments
    Which reaches the very dust;
It can touch the stains
Of the streets and the lanes;
    And because it can it must.

I ought to bend to the lowest,
    I ought, and therefore I can;
I was made to the end
That I might descend
    In the steps of the Son of Man.

— Author unknown

I Want to Sing Lyrics

I want to sing lyrics, lyrics,
  Mad as a brook in spring.
I want to shout the music
  Of flushed adventuring.

But how can I sing lyrics?
  I who have seen today
The stoop of factory women,
  And children kept from play.

And on an open hilltop,
  Where the cloak of the sky is wide,
Have seen a tree of terror
  Where a black man died.

I want to sing lyrics, lyrics,
  But these have hushed my song.
I am mute at the world's great sadness,
  And stark at the world's great wrong.

— *Author unknown*

LOOKING UNTO JESUS

Since Christ the Saviour I have known
My rules are all reduced to one,
To keep my Lord, by faith, in view;
This strength supplies, and motives, too.

To look to Jesus as He rose,
Confirms my faith, disarms my foes,
Satan I shame and overcome,
By pointing to my Saviour's tomb.

Exalted on His glorious throne,
I see Him make my cause His own;
Then all my anxious cares subside,
For Jesus lives and will provide.

By faith I see the hour at hand,
When in His presence I shall stand;
Then it will be my endless bliss
To see Him where and as He is.

— John Newton

God's Sunshine

Never once since the world began
    Has the sun ever stopped his shining.
His face very often we could not see,
And we grumbled at his inconstancy;
But the clouds were really to blame, not he,
    For, behind them, he was shining.

And so — behind life's darkest clouds
    God's love is always shining.
We veil it at times with our faithless fears,
And darken our sight with our foolish tears,
But in time the atmosphere always clears,
    For his love is always shining.

— *John Oxenham*

Let Me Hear Thee

O let me hear Thee speaking,
    In accents clear and still,
Above the storms of passion,
    The murmurs of self-will;
O speak to reassure me,
    To hasten or control;
O speak, and make me listen,
    Thou Guardian of my soul.

— *John Ernest Bode*

Know and Knowing Not

He who knows not,
And knows not that he knows not,
    Is a fool — shun him.

He who knows not,
And knows that he knows not,
    Is humble — teach him.

He who knows
And knows not that he knows,
    Is asleep — wake him.

He who knows
And knows that he knows,
    Is wise — follow him.

— Author unknown

Thou Art the Way

Thou art the Way; to Thee alone
    From sin and death we flee;
And he who would the Father seek,
    Must seek Him, Lord, by Thee.

Thou art the Truth; Thy word alone
    True wisdom can impart;
Thou only canst inform the mind,
    And purify the heart.

Thou art the Life; the rending tomb
    Proclaims Thy conquering arm;
And those who put their trust in Thee
    Nor death nor hell shall harm.

Thou art the Way, the Truth, the Life;
    Grant us that Way to know,
That Truth to keep, that Life to win,
    Whose joys eternal flow.

— Bishop Doane

USE ME, GOD

Use me, God, in Thy great harvest field,
Which stretcheth far and wide like a wide sea;
The gatherers are so few; I fear the precious yield
Will suffer loss. Oh, find a place for me!
A place where best the strength I have will tell;
It may be one the older toilers shun;
Be it a wide or narrow place, 'tis well
So that the work it holds be only done.

— *Christina Rossetti*

TIME

Time is money — we have no right to waste it.
Time is power — we have no right to dissipate it.
Time is influence — we have no right to throw it away.
Time is life — we must value it greatly.
Time is God's — He gives it to us for a purpose.
Time is a sacred trust — we must answer for every moment.
Time is wisdom — we have no right to be ignorant.
Time is preparation for eternity — we must redeem it.

— *Author unknown*

WE ARE READY

Ready to go, ready to wait,
  Ready a gap to fill!
Ready for service, small or great,
  Ready to do His will.

Ready to suffer grief or pain,
  Ready to stand the test!
Ready to stay at home and send
  Others, if He sees best!

Ready to do, ready to bear,
  Ready to watch and pray!
Ready to stand aside and give
  Till He shall clear the way!

Ready to speak, ready to think,
  Ready with heart and brain;
Ready to stand where He sees fit,
  Ready to share the strain!

Ready to seek, ready to warn,
  Ready o'er souls to yearn!
Ready in life, ready in death,
  Ready for His return!

— C. Palmer

The Preacher's Prayer

Let me be a little kinder,
Let me be a little blinder
To the fault of those about me;
Let me praise a little more;
Let me be, when I am weary,
Just a little bit more cheery;
Let me serve a little better
Those that I am striving for.

Let me be a little braver,
When temptation bids me waver;
Let me strive a little harder
To be all that I should be;
Let me be a little meeker
With the brother that is weaker;
Let me think more of my people
And a little less of me.

— *Author unknown*

QUESTIONS

The same old baffling questions! O my friend
I cannot answer them.
I have no answer for myself or thee
Save what I learned beside my mother's knee:
All is of God that is and is to be;
And God is good. Let this suffice us still,
Resting in childlike trust upon His will
Who moves to His great purposes unthwarted by the ill.

— *William Cowper*

PURPOSE

Find out what God would have you do
 And do that little well,
For what is great and what is small
 'Tis only He can tell.

— *Author unknown*

THREE WAYS TO LOOK

Would you be troubled, look within;
Would you be distracted, look around;
Would you be restful, look above.

— *News Bulletin*

No Pocket in a Shroud

Use your money while you're living,
Do not hoard it to be proud;
You can never take it with you —
There's no pocket in a shroud.

Gold can help you on no farther
Than the graveyard where you lie,
And though you are rich while living
You're a pauper when you die.

Use it then some lives to brighten,
As through life they weary plod;
Place your bank account in heaven
And grow richer toward your God.

Use it wisely, use it freely,
Do not hoard it to be proud;
You can never take it with you —
There's no pocket in a shroud.

— *Author unknown*

I Am Continually With Thee

Sometimes I feel quite lonely,
   So many dear ones gone;
And the way seems all the harder,
   Because it is so long.
Until a gentle whisper —
   So sweetly speaks to me,
"Nevertheless, I am continually with thee."

Continually, dear Master,
   Continually with me;
Then I can need no other,
   Though dark the path may be,
For Thou hast set the pathway,
   Wherein my feet should tread,
And walking close beside Thee
   I shall be safely led.

How can I fear the darkness?
   How can I feel alone?
When Thou, my precious Saviour,
   Hast made me all Thine own.
I've only just to trust Thee,
   And hear Thee say to me —
"Nevertheless, I am continually with thee."

"Nevertheless, I am continually with thee."
   How wonderful that God
Should walk and talk with me.
   "My presence shall go with thee,
And I will give thee rest,"
   Is just another promise —
By which my soul is blest.
   "Lo, I am with you alway, even unto the end."
A wondrous, threefold promise,
   From Christ, my living Friend.

— *Author unknown*

My Guide

He who from zone to zone,
Guides through the boundless sky thy certain flight,
In the long way that I must tread alone,
    Will lead my steps aright.

— William Cullen Bryant

Teach Us to Pray

O Thou, by whom we come to God,
    The Life, the Truth, the Way;
The path of prayer Thyself hast trod;
    Teach us how to pray.

— James Montgomery

Keep on Keeping On

The harder the thing is to do
   The greater the joy when it's done,
The farther the goal is from you
   The sweeter the thrill when it's won.

The deeper the problem, the more
   Is the joy when you've puzzled it out;
The seas that run fartherest from shore
   Are only for ships that are stout.

Men weary of lessons they've learned
   And tire of the tasks they can do.
Life it seems is forever concerned
   With blazing a path to the new.

So stand to the worry and care.
   Everlastingly keep going on.
The greater the burden you bear,
   The greater the joy when it's done.

— Author unknown

Imprinted Images

Walk in the starlight long enough
  And the silver will touch your hair,
For the stars will lean from heaven
  And be reflected there.

Talk with the angels long enough
  And your very face will shine,
For the peace of God will touch your eyes
  With radiance divine.

Only give God and the angels time
  To burnish what once was dim,
And the glory may rest on all of us,
  For was it not so with Him?

— Author unknown

GIVE, GIVE

Give, give, be always giving.
Who gives not, does not live.
The more we give
The more we live.

— *Author unknown*

A LITTLE LIGHT

God make my life a little light
  Within the world to glow,
A little flame that burneth bright
  Wherever I may go.

— *M. Betham Edwards*

You Tell on Yourself

You tell what you are by the friends you seek,
By the very manner in which you speak,
By the way you employ your leisure time,
By the use you make of dollar and dime.

You tell what you are by the things you wear,
By the spirit in which you burdens bear,
By the kind of things at which you laugh,
By records you play on the phonograph.

You tell what you are by the way you walk,
By the things of which you delight to talk,
By the manner in which you bear defeat,
By so simple a thing as how you eat.

By the books you choose from the well-filled shelf;
In these ways and more, you tell on yourself,
So there's really no particle of sense
In an effort to keep up false pretense.

— *Author unknown*

LEST WE FORGET

God of our fathers, known of old,
   Lord of our far-flung battle-line,
Beneath whose awful hand we hold
   Dominion over palm and pine —
Lord God of hosts, be with us yet,
Lest we forget — lest we forget!

The tumult and the shouting dies;
   The captains and the kings depart:
Still stands Thine ancient sacrifice,
   An humble and a contrite heart.
Lord God of hosts, be with us yet,
Lest we forget — lest we forget!

Far-called, our navies melt away,
   On dune and headland sinks the fire:
Lo, all our pomp of yesterday
   Is one with Nineveh and Tyre!
Judge of the nations, spare us yet,
Lest we forget — lest we forget!

If, drunk with sight of power, we loose
   Wild tongues that have not Thee in awe,
Such boastings as the Gentiles use,
   Or lesser breeds without the law —
Lord God of hosts, be with us yet,
Lest we forget — lest we forget!

For heathen heart that puts her trust
   In reeking tube and iron shard,
All valiant dust that builds on dust
   And guarding, calls not Thee to guard,
For frantic boast and foolish word —
Thy mercy on Thy people, Lord!

          — *Rudyard Kipling*

God's Word

No book is like the Bible
    For childhood, youth, and age;
Our duty plain and simple
    We find on every page.
It came by inspiration,
    A light to guide our way,
A voice from Him who gave it
    Reproving when we stray.

— Fanny J. Crosby

Teach Me

Teach me, dear Lord, what Thou wouldst have me know;
Guide me, dear Lord, where Thou wouldst have me go;
Help me, dear Lord, the precious seed to sow;
Bless Thou the seed that it may surely grow.

— Author unknown

Forgive and Forget

Oh, forgive and forget! for this life is too fleeting
  To waste it in brooding o'er wrongs we have met;
It is better, far better, to smother our anger,
  To teach the proud heart to forgive and forget.

Then forgive and forget! if the friends you love fondly,
  Prove themselves false and unworthy of trust,
Deal with them kindly, for they are but mortals,
  Erring like us, for we are but dust.

Deal with them tenderly, pity their weakness.
  We know every heart hath its evil and good;
One Father in heaven we have, hence we are brothers:
  Then let us forgive and forget as we should.

— Author unknown

A Simple Trust

Faith is a very simple thing,
  Though little understood;
It frees the soul from death's dread sting
  By resting in the blood.

Faith is not what we feel or see,
  It is a simple trust
In what the God of love has said
  Of Jesus as "the Just."

What Jesus is and that alone,
  Is faith's delightful plea;
It never deals with sinful self,
  Nor righteous self in me.

It tells me I am counted "dead"
  By God in His own Word;
It tells me I am "born again"
  In Christ, my risen Lord.

If He is free, then I am free
  From all unrighteousness;
If He is just, then I am just,
  He is my righteousness.

— *Author unknown*

CONQUERORS

We never need be vanquished,
    We never need give in,
Though waging war with Satan
    And compassed round by sin;
Temptations will beset us,
    Allurement oft assail,
But in the name of Jesus
    We shall, we must prevail.

— *Author unknown*

MY SAVIOUR'S LOVE

Wide, wide as the ocean,
High as the heavens above,
Deep, deep as the deepest sea
Is my Saviour's love;
I, though so unworthy,
Still am a child of His care,
For His Word teaches me
That His love reaches me
    Everywhere.

— *Author unknown*

A LIVING, BRIGHT REALITY

Lord Jesus, make Thyself to me
A living, bright reality;
More pleasant to faith's vision keen
Than any outward object seen;
More dear, more intimately nigh.
Than e'en the sweetest earthly tie.

— Author unknown

LIVE WELL TODAY

Yesterday is already a dream,
And tomorrow is only a vision;
But today, well lived, makes
Every yesterday a dream of happiness,
And every tomorrow a vision of hope.

— From the Sanscrit

LIFE'S LESSONS

I learn as the years roll onward
    And I leave the past behind,
That much I have counted sorrow
    But proves that God is kind;
That many a flower I'd longed for
    Had hidden a thorn of pain,
And many a rugged by-path
    Led to fields of ripened grain.

The clouds that cover the sunshine,
    They cannot banish the sun,
And the earth shines out the brighter
    When the weary rain is done.
We must stand in the deepest shadow
    To see the clearest light;
And often through wrong's own darkness
    Comes the living strength of light.

The sweetest rest is at even,
    After a wearisome day,
When the heavy burden of labor
    Has been borne from our hearts away;
And those who have ne'er known sorrow
    Cannot know the infinite peace
That falls on a troubled spirit
    When it sees at last release.

We must live through the dreary Winter
    If we would value the Spring;
And the woods must be cold and silent
    Before the robins sing;
The flowers must be buried in darkness
    Before they can bud and bloom,
And the sweetest, warmest sunshine
    Comes after the storm and gloom.

— Anonymous

GOD AND HOME

God is in every tomorrow.
  Life with its changes may come;
He is behind and before me,
  While in the distance shines home.
Home, where no thought of tomorrow
  Ever can shadow my brow.
Home — in the presence of Jesus.
  Thru all eternity, now.

A message comes in the heartache,
  A whisper of love in the pain,
The pangs we have fought and conquered
  Tell the sweet story of gain.
So it comes to me more and more
  As I enter on each new day,
The love of the Father Eternal,
  Is over us all the way.

— *Author unknown*

REST IN THE LORD

Rest in the Lord, my soul;
　Commit to Him thy way.
What to thy sight seems dark as night
　To Him is bright as day.

Rest in the Lord, my soul;
　He planned for thee thy life.
Brings fruit from rain, brings good from pain
　And peace and joy from strife.

Rest in the Lord, my soul;
　This fretting weakens thee,
Why not be still, accept His will?
　Thou shalt His glory see.

— Author unknown

God Meant It for Good

Until I learned to trust
  I never learned to pray;
And I did not learn to fully trust
  'Til sorrows came my way.

Until I felt my weakness
  His strength I never knew;
Nor dreamed 'til I was stricken
  That He could see me through.

Who deepest drinks of sorrow
  Drinks deepest, too, of grace;
He sends the storm so He himself
  Can be our hiding place.

His heart, that seeks our highest good
  Knows well when things annoy;
We would not long for heaven
  If earth held only joy.

— *Author unknown*

SALVATION

Not what these hands have done
    Can save this guilty soul;
Not what this toiling flesh has borne
    Can make my spirit whole.

Not what I feel or do
    Can give me peace with God;
Not all my prayers, my sighs, my tears,
    Can bear my awful load.

Thy work alone, O Christ,
    Can ease this weight of sin;
Thy blood alone, O Lamb of God,
    Can give me peace within.

— Horatius Bonar

PERFECT REDEMPTION

Oh, perfect redemption the purchase of blood,
    To every believer the promise of God;
The vilest offender who fully believes,
    That moment from Jesus a pardon receives.

— Fanny J. Crosby

My Purpose

To be a little kindlier
  With the passing of each day;
To leave but happy memories
  As I go along my way;
To use possessions that are mine
  In service full and free;
To sacrifice the trivial things
  For larger good to be;
To give of love in lavish way
  That friendships true may live;
To be less quick to criticize,
  More ready to forgive;
To use such talents as I have
  That happiness may grow;
To take the bitter with the sweet,
  Assured 'tis better so;
To be quite free from self-intent
  Whate'er the task I do;
To help the world's faith stronger grow
  In all that's good and true;
To keep my faith in God and right
  No matter how things run.
To work and play and pray and trust
  Until the journey's done.
God grant to me the strength of heart,
  Of motive and of will,
To do my part, and falter not
  This purpose to fulfil.

— Author unknown

I See My Faults

I have so many faults myself,
I seldom see
A defect in another's life,
But what I see in me;
I make so many fool mistakes
I feel condemned to find
A bit of fault in anyone
When I'm so far behind.
I used to censure everyone,
I was a Pharisee;
Until quite unexpectedly
I got a glimpse of me.
I tried to justify myself
And frame some alibi;
But here I stood caught by myself
And I to me would lie.
And whenever I'm inclined
Some other's judge to be,
I always go and take a look
At him whom I call me.
I find it is a splendid thing.
Just try it and you'll see —
To keep from criticizing folks,
Let each I look at me.

—Author unknown

SAFETY

O Lord, it is a blessed thing
To Thee both morn and night to bring
Our worship's lowly offering.

And, from the strife of tongues away,
Ere toil begins, to meet and pray
For blessings on the coming day.

O Jesus, be our morning Light,
That we may go forth to the fight
With strength renewed and armour bright.

And when our daily work is o'er
And sins and weakness we deplore,
Oh, then be Thou our Light once more.

Light of the world! with us abide,
And to Thyself our footsteps guide
At morn, and noon, and eventide.

—Bishop How

O God, Look Down From Heaven

O God, look down from heaven, we pray,
  Thy tenderness awaken!
Thy saints so few, fade fast away,
  Hast Thou Thy poor forsaken?
Thy Word no more is taught aright,
And faith from earth hath vanished quite —
  O Lord, our God, revive us.

— Martin Luther

Christ, My All in All

O Christ, my all in all Thou art,
My rest in toil, my ease in pain;
The balm to heal my broken heart;
In storms my peace, in loss my gain;
My joy beneath the worldling's frown;
In shame, my glory and my crown.
In want, my plentiful supply;
In weakness, mine almighty power;
In bonds, my perfect liberty;
My refuge in temptation's hour;
My comfort 'midst all grief and pain,
My life in death, my endless gain.

— Author unknown

FAITH'S POWER

Father of Jesus Christ, my Lord,
  My Saviour and my Head,
I trust in Thee, whose powerful Word
  Hath raised Him from the dead.

In hope, against all human hope,
  Self desperate, I believe;
Thy quickening Word shall raise me up,
  Thou wilt thy spirit give.

Faith, mighty faith, the promise sees,
  And looks to that alone;
Laughs at impossibilities,
  And cries, "It shall be done!"

To Thee the glory of Thy power
  And faithfulness I give,
I shall in Christ, at that glad hour,
  And Christ in me shall live.

Obedient faith, that waits on Thee,
  Thou never wilt reprove;
But Thou wilt form Thy Son in me,
  And perfect me in love.

— *Charles Wesley*

POWER THROUGH COMMUNION

Lo, what a change within us one short hour
    Spent in Thy presence will prevail to make,
    What heavy burdens from our bosom take,
What parched grounds revive as with a shower;
We kneel, and all around us seems to lower;
    We rise, and all, the distant and the near,
    Stands forth in sunny outline, brave and clear;
We kneel, how weak; we rise, how full of power!

                   — *Archbishop Trench*

GIVE US HEARTS TO LOVE

Thy foes might hate, despise, revile,
    Thy friends unfaithful prove,
Unwearied in forgiveness still,
    Thy heart could only love.
O give us hearts to love like Thee,
    Like Thee, O Lord, to grieve
Far more for others' sins than all
    The wrongs that we receive.

                   — *Author unknown*

Draw Out Now

All I have is thine,
For thee My blood was spilt;
Thy every need I can supply,
Draw out just what thou wilt.

Is it lack of love
For dying souls around?
Draw out My deeper love
And in that love abound.

Why hast thou little power
In that great work of thine
When all I have is now for thee?
Draw out My power divine.

Why hast thou little joy?
Oh! now arise and shine;
I would not have thee sad, My child,
Draw now this joy divine.

What dost thou lack, beloved?
Whene'er, whate'er it be
Remember all that I have is thine —
Draw out now all from Me.

— *Author unknown*

SAFELY ABIDING

Who trusts in God, a strong abode
    In Heaven and earth possesses;
Who looks in love to Christ above,
    No fear his heart oppresses.
In Thee alone, dear Lord, we own
    Sweet hope and consolation;
Our shield from foes, our balm for woes,
    Our great and sure salvation.

Though Satan's wrath beset our path,
    And worldly scorn assail us,
While Thou art near we will not fear,
    Thy strength shall never fail us:
Thy rod and staff shall keep us safe,
    And guide our steps for ever;
Nor shades of death, nor hell beneath,
    Our souls from Thee shall sever.

In all the strife of mortal life
    Our feet shall stand securely;
Temptation's hour shall lose its power,
    For Thou shalt guard us surely.
O God, renew, with heavenly dew,
    Our body, soul, and spirit,
Until we stand at Thy right hand,
    Through Jesus' saving merit.

— Joachim Magdeburg
    Trans. by Benj. Kennedy;
    Altered by Wm. Walsham How

Not Death to Die

It is not death to die,
　To leave this weary load,
And with the brotherhood on high
　To be at home with God.

— Author unknown

Look to Him

Look to Him Who ever liveth,
Interceding for His own;
Seek, yea, claim the grace He giveth
Freely from His priestly throne.
Will He not thy strength renew
With His Spirit's quickening dew?

Look to Him, and faith shall brighten,
Hope shall soar, and love shall burn,
Peace once more thy heart shall lighten.
Rise! He calleth thee; return!
Be not weary on thy way.
For He is thy strength and stay.

— Author unknown

THOUSAND, THOUSAND THANKS

Christ, the Life of all the living,
 Christ, the Death of death, our foe,
Who Thyself for me once giving
 To the darkest depths of woe,
Patiently didst yield Thy breath
But to save my soul from death;
Thousand, thousand thanks shall be
 O Lord Jesus, unto Thee.

Thou didst bear the smiting only
 That it might not fall on me;
Stoodest falsely charged and lonely
 That I might be safe and free;
Comfortless that I might know
 Comfort from Thy boundless woe;
Thousand, thousand thanks shall be,
 O Lord Jesus, unto Thee.

      — From the German

A Way

To every man there openeth
A way and ways and a way;
The high soul climbs the high way,
And the low soul gropes for the low,
And in between on the misty flats
The rest drift to and fro.
To every man there openeth
A high way and a low
And every man decideth
The way his soul shall go.

— *Author unknown*

Omnipotence

Say not, my soul, "from whence
    Can God relieve my care?"
Remember that Omnipotence
    Has servants everywhere.
His wisdom is sublime,
    His heart profoundly kind:
    God is never before His time,
    And never is behind.

— *Author unknown*

CASTING CARE ON GOD

Should Thy mercy send me
Sorrow, toil, and woe;
Or should pain attend me
On my path below;
Grant that I may never
Fail Thy hand to see;
Grant that I may ever
Cast my care on Thee.

— *James Montgomery*

GOD'S SMILE

In trouble, and in grief, O God,
  Thy smile has cheered my way;
And joy has budded from each thorn
  Which round my pathway lay.
The hours of pain have yielded good
  Which prosperous days refused;
Like herbs, though scentless when entire,
  Spread fragrance when they're bruised.

— *Author unknown*

No Fancies

Since, Lord, Thou dost defend
   Us with Thy Spirit
We know we at the end
   Shall life inherit.
Then fancies flee away!
   I'll fear not what men say,
I'll labor night and day
   To be a pilgrim.

— *John Bunyan*

Take Thou Our Hearts

Take Thou our hearts, and let them be
Forever closed to all but Thee;
Thy willing servants, let us wear
The seal of love forever there.

How blest are they who still abide
Close sheltered in Thy loving side;
Who life and strength from Thee receive,
And with Thee move, and in Thee live.

— *Selected*

Jesus Is All

When creature comforts fade and die,
Worldlings may weep, but why should I?
Jesus still lives, and still is nigh.

Though all the flocks and herds were dead,
My soul a famine need not dread,
For Jesus is my living bread.

I know not what may soon betide,
Or how my wants shall be supplied;
But Jesus knows and will provide.

Against me earth and hell combine,
But on my side is power divine,
Jesus is all, and He is mine.

— Selected

My Jesus, As Thou Wilt

My Jesus, as Thou wilt!
O may Thy will be mine;
Into Thy hand of love
I would my all resign;
Through sorrow or through joy,
Conduct me as Thine own,
And help me still to say,
My Lord, Thy will be done!

My Jesus, as Thou wilt!
All shall be well with me;
Each changing future scene
I gladly trust with Thee;
Straight to my home above
I travel calmly on,
And sing in life or death,
My Lord, Thy will be done!

— *Benjamin Schmolck*